What Did Dinosaurs Eat?

And Other Things You Want to Know About Dinosaurs

Written by
Elizabeth MacLeod

Illustrated by
Gordon Sauvé

Kids Can Press

For Matthew Jordan,
... as fierce as a Tyrannosaurus
... as gentle as a Maiasaura

Many thanks to Dr. Philip J. Currie, Head, Dinosaur Research Program and Curator of Dinosaurs and Birds, Royal Tyrrell Museum, for reading an early draft of this book.

Kids Can Press acknowledges the financial support of the Ontario Arts Council, the Canada Council for the Arts and the Government of Canada, through the BPIDP, for our publishing activity.

Published in Canada by	Published in the U.S. by
Kids Can Press Ltd.	Kids Can Press Ltd.
29 Birch Avenue	2250 Military Road
Toronto, ON M4V 1E2	Tonawanda, NY 14150

www.kidscanpress.com

The artwork in this book was rendered in acrylic paints.
The text is set in Century Gothic.

Edited by Lori Burwash
Designed by Julia Naimska
Printed in Hong Kong by Wing King Tong Company Limited

This book is smyth sewn casebound.

CM 01 0 9 8 7 6 5 4 3 2 1

National Library of Canada Cataloguing in Publication Data

MacLeod, Elizabeth
What did dinosaurs eat? : and other things you want to know about dinosaurs

ISBN 1-55337-063-5

1. Dinosaurs — Miscellanea — Juvenile literature. I. Sauvé, Gordon. II. Title.

QE861.5.M32 2001   j567.9   C2001-930161-8

Kids Can Press is a Nelvana company

Contents

What is a dinosaur?

Many things make an animal a dinosaur. First, it lived 225 million to 65 million years ago. Its legs were also right under its body. They did not stick out, like a lizard's. As well, a dinosaur could not swim. But experts think that some could fly.

Apatosaurus is one of the best-known dinosaurs. This dinosaur's body was longer than two school buses. You could lie down in its footprint.

How big were dinosaurs?

Dinosaurs came in all sizes. Some were as tall as a house. Others weighed more than six elephants. But there were also dinosaurs that weighed less than a cat. They were so small that you could have held them in your arms.

Seismosaurus was the longest dinosaur. It was about half as long as a football field.

Compsognathus was the smallest dinosaur. It was about the same size as a chicken.

What did dinosaurs eat?

Most dinosaurs ate plants. They snacked on flowers, fern-like plants and huge evergreen trees. Other dinosaurs ate meat. They munched insects, birds, fish, eggs and other dinosaurs. Some dinosaurs ate both plants and meat.

Tyrannosaurus was one of the biggest meat-eating dinosaurs. Its teeth were as long as bananas! *Tyrannosaurus* was always hungry. It would even eat smelly dead dinosaurs.

Were dinosaurs smart?

Dinosaurs were smart enough to hunt or find food. They could also raise their babies and escape from enemies. Most dinosaurs were as smart as today's lizards and crocodiles.

Troodon was probably the smartest dinosaur. It had the biggest brain of any dinosaur, compared to the size of its body. It was as smart as some birds and smarter than any lizard.

How fast could dinosaurs run?

The fastest dinosaurs could run faster than a car driving on a city street. They looked a little like ostriches. Other dinosaurs were very slow. The big, heavy dinosaurs with short legs were probably the slowest.

Gallimimus was one of the
fastest dinosaurs. It had
to run quickly to catch
the animals and insects it
gobbled. *Gallimimus* used
its small, clawed hands to
grab its dinner.

What color were dinosaurs?

Dinosaurs probably came in all colors, just like animals and birds today. Perhaps some were brightly colored. Others might have blended into the dirt and sand around them. Dinosaurs could have had spots or stripes, too.

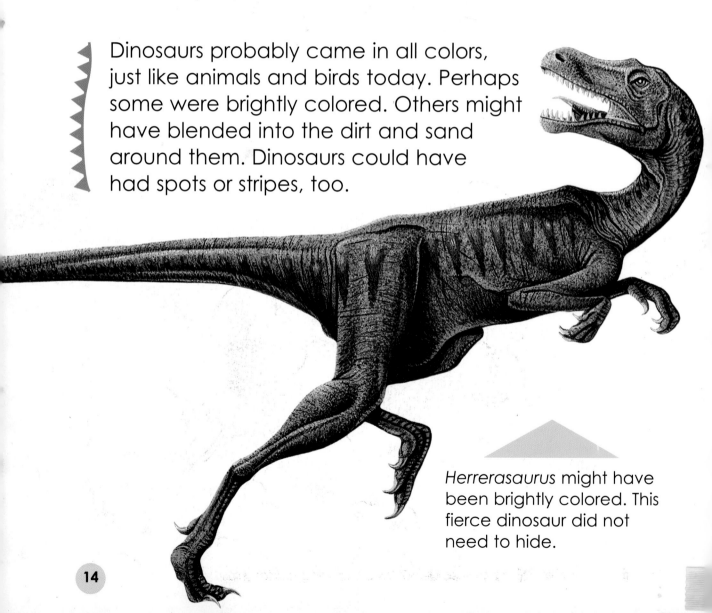

Herrerasaurus might have been brightly colored. This fierce dinosaur did not need to hide.

Slow, awkward *Euoplocephalus* might have had drab skin to help it hide from enemies. If it had to fight, this dinosaur used the club on its tail.

In real life, *Euoplocephalus* was about twice as long as *Herrerasaurus*.

What did dinosaurs sound like?

Experts guess that dinosaurs sounded like today's animals. They probably honked or hooted to call to other dinosaurs. When they fought, they snarled and roared. Perhaps some dinosaurs snorted or squawked to find a mate.

The crest on the head of a *Parasaurolophus* was about the size of a baseball bat. This dinosaur used the crest to make its long, low call.

How were baby dinosaurs born?

Baby dinosaurs hatched from eggs. Some dinosaurs laid their eggs on the ground and left them to hatch on their own. Other dinosaurs laid their eggs in shallow pits that they dug themselves. They probably cared for their babies after they hatched.

A mother *Maiasaura* laid her eggs in a nest. She carefully covered the eggs with sand and plants. After they hatched, the babies probably lived in the nest for many months.

How long could a dinosaur live?

The biggest dinosaurs lived the longest. Some of the largest were probably hundreds of years old! A dinosaur as big as a man was about 15 to 20 years old. Smaller dinosaurs had shorter lives.

It might have taken *Diplodocus* 200 years to grow this big. This dinosaur was one of the largest ever. It weighed more than four elephants.

Were all dinosaurs fierce?

Some dinosaurs were fierce hunters. Many had long claws and sharp, jagged teeth to rip and chew their food. Other dinosaurs were shy plant eaters. They had flat teeth to grind their food. To stay safe, these dinosaurs traveled in herds or hid from their enemies.

Deinonychus was one of the fiercest dinosaurs. It had big jaws full of long teeth. This fast, smart dinosaur used its sharp claws to rip into its dinner.

Could dinosaurs fly?

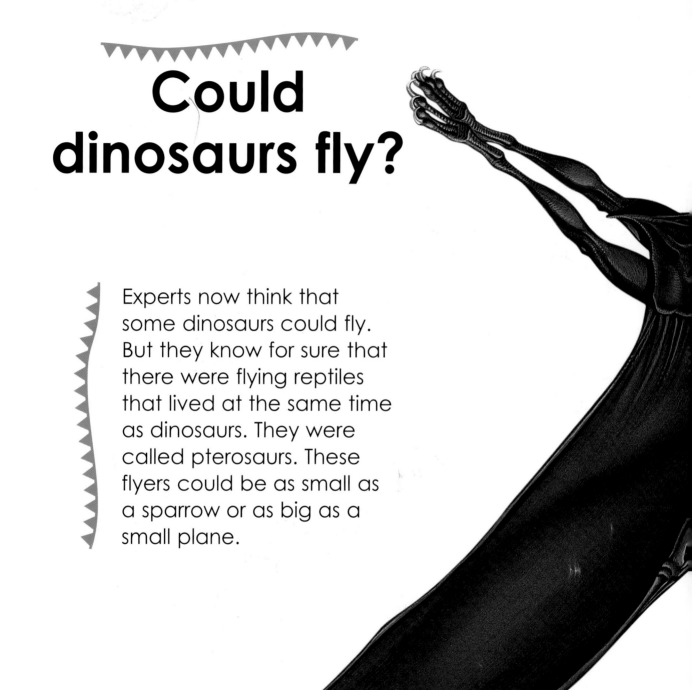

Experts now think that some dinosaurs could fly. But they know for sure that there were flying reptiles that lived at the same time as dinosaurs. They were called pterosaurs. These flyers could be as small as a sparrow or as big as a small plane.

Quetzalcoatlus was the biggest pterosaur. It had excellent eyesight and could spot animals and fish far below. This huge flyer would swoop down and scoop up its dinner.

What happened to the dinosaurs?

Many scientists think that most dinosaurs died when an asteroid hit Earth. Steam and dust blocked out the sunlight. Plants and animals, including dinosaurs, died.

Other scientists also say that some meat-eating dinosaurs evolved into birds. This change took millions of years.

Dinosaurs such as *Coelophysis*
might have evolved into birds.
Some experts even think that
this dinosaur had feathers.
Coelophysis was small and fast.

Where do scientists find dinosaur bones?

Dinosaur bones are found around the world. They have even been found in the Arctic! Scientists look for bones in rock that is as old as the bones. Sometimes bones are easy to spot because they stick out of rocky cliffs. But sometimes scientists must dig deep in the ground to find bones.

Scientists have found
many good skeletons of
Stegosaurus. They think
that this dinosaur used
the plates on its back to
warm and cool itself.

What can dinosaur bones tell scientists?

Dinosaur bones tell scientists many things. Growth rings in the bones show how old a dinosaur was. Bumps or growths on a bone can mean that the dinosaur had arthritis or bone cancer. And broken tail bones show that some dinosaurs were clumsy and stepped on one another.

The skull bones of *Pachycephalosaurus* are very thick. This makes scientists think that it used its head to butt other dinosaurs

Triceratops probably used their huge horns for fighting each other. Scientists have found horn-sized holes in the neck frills and skulls of this dinosaur.

In real life, *Triceratops* was about twice as long as *Pachycephalosaurus*.

Dinosaur names

Did you know that dinosaur means "terrible lizard"?

Name	How to say it	What it means
Apatosaurus	Ah-PAT-uh-SORE-us	Deceptive lizard
(Experts confused this dinosaur's bones with another's — the bones "deceived" them.)		
Coelophysis	SEE-loh-FY-sis	Hollow form
(When this dinosaur was named, it was not known that many had hollow bones.)		
Compsognathus	Komp-so-NAY-thus	Pretty jaw
Deinonychus	Dye-NON-uh-kus	Terrible claw
Diplodocus	Dih-PLOD-uh-kus	Double-beamed
(This dinosaur's tail had extra, or double, bones.)		
Euoplocephalus	You-oh-pluh-SEF-uh-lus	Well-armored head
Gallimimus	Gal-uh-MEE-mus	Chicken mimic
(This dinosaur looked a bit like a chicken.)		
Herrerasaurus	Huh-RARE-uh-SORE-us	Herrera's lizard
(A man named Victorino Herrera discovered this dinosaur's bones.)		
Maiasaura	My-ah-SORE-uh	Good mother lizard
Pachycephalosaurus	PACK-ee-SEF-ah-lo-SORE-us	Thick-headed lizard
Parasaurolophus	PAIR-ah-SORE-all-uh-FUS	Like crested lizard
Quetzalcoatlus	KWET-zel-kwat-lus	Feathered serpent
(This reptile was a pterosaur — TARE-uh-sore — which means winged lizard.)		
Seismosaurus	Size-mo-SORE-us	Earthquake lizard
Stegosaurus	Steg-uh-SORE-us	Roof lizard
(Experts thought that this dinosaur's back plates lay flat, like roof shingles.)		
Triceratops	Try-SARE-uh-TOPS	Three-horned face
Troodon	TROH-uh-don	Wounding tooth
Tyrannosaurus	Tie-RAN-uh-SORE-us	Tyrant lizard

Web sites

www.enchantedlearning.com/subjects/dinosaurs/index.html
www.discovery.com/exp/fossilzone/sounds/dinosounds.html
www.sdnhm.org/kids/dinosaur